LIVING AND WORKING TOGETHER

ALL ABOUT YOU

BOOK 1

Senior Author
Dahia Shabaka

**Published by
Metropolitan Teaching
and Learning Company**

Reginald Powe
President

Juwanda G. Ford
Managing Editor

Copyright ©1999 Metropolitan Teaching and Learning Company. Published by Metropolitan Teaching and Learning Company. All rights reserved. No part of this book may be reproduced or transmitted in any form or by any means, electronic or mechanical, including photocopying and recording, or by any information storage or retrieval system without prior written permission of the Metropolitan Teaching and Learning Company unless such copying is expressly permitted under federal copyright law.

For information regarding permission, write to the address below.

Metropolitan Teaching and Learning Company
33 Irving Place
New York, NY 10003

ISBN: 1-58120-826-X

2 3 4 5 6 7 8 9 10 CL 05 04 03 02 01

Book 1

ALL ABOUT YOU

There is no one like me.
There is no one like you.
We are all special.

LESSON 1 — YOU ARE SPECIAL

You wear your hair in different ways.

You wear different styles of clothes.

You each have fun in different ways.

You each can do special things. You are special!

What is special about you?

LESSON 2 YOUR NAME

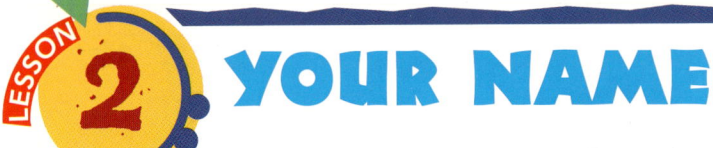

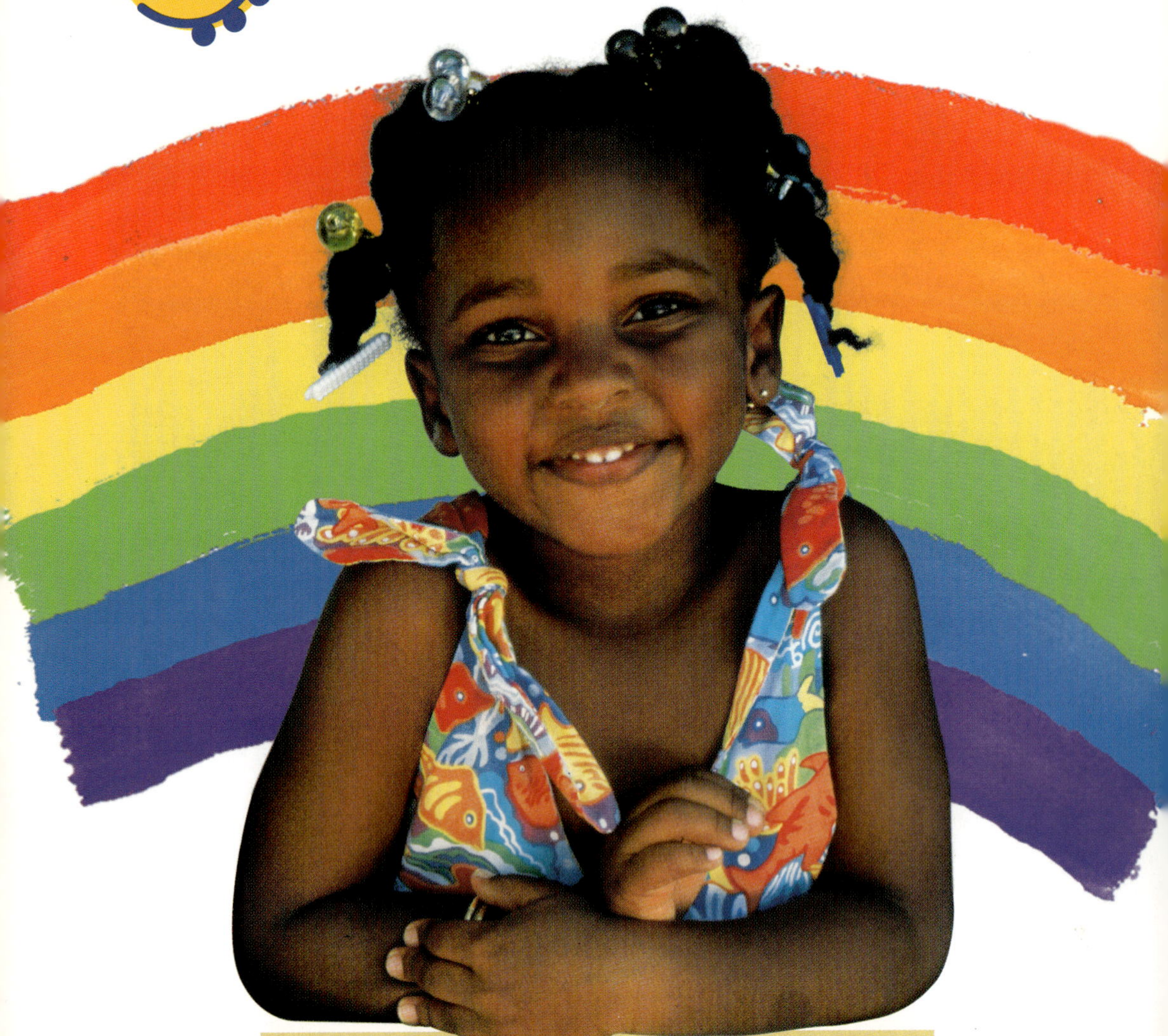

Names are special, too.
This is Ayeola.
Ayeola is an African name.
It means "rainbow."

This is Reggie.
Reggie is an English name.
It means "king."

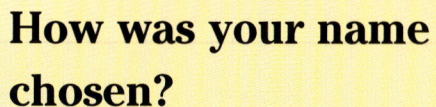

How was your name chosen?

SKILLS LESSON

Book 1

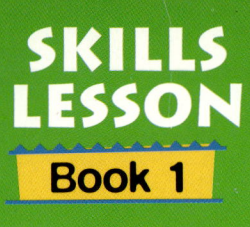

Days of the Week

Hello.

My name is Miguel.

These are the days in my week.

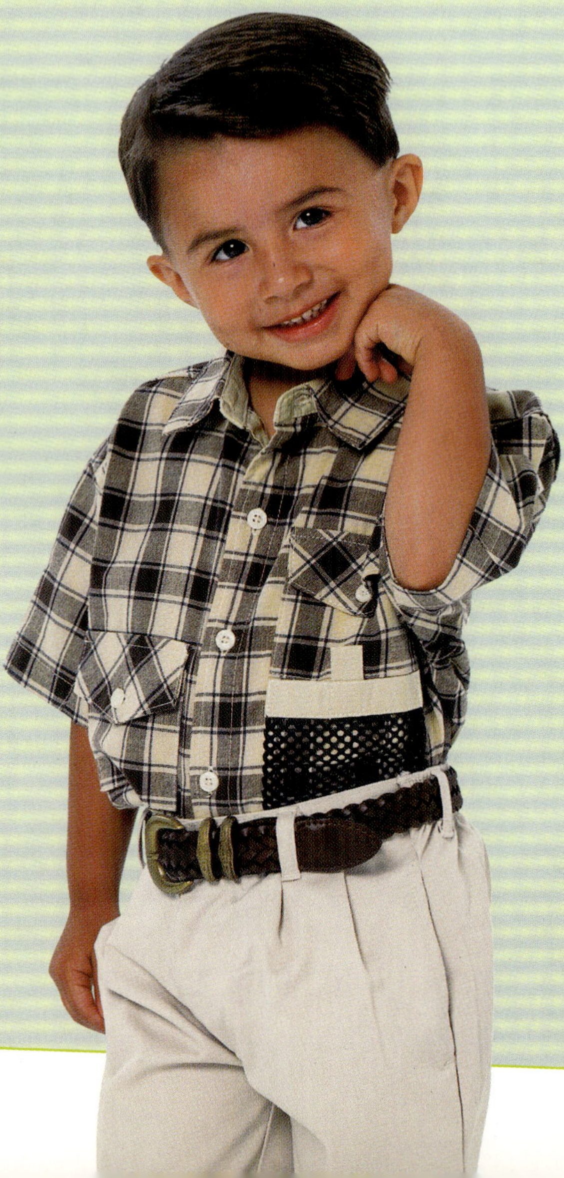

SUNDAY

MONDAY

TUESDAY

WEDNESDAY

THURSDAY

FRIDAY

SATURDAY

LESSON 3 YOU BELONG TO A FAMILY

The Johnson family has a mother, father, brother, and sister. Each of them is special.

The Hue family has a father and a son.
Both of them are special, too.

Uncle John

Grandma Ellie

In a small family, everyone is special.
In a big family, everyone is special, too.

Cousin Rosa

 Who is special in your family?

LESSON 4 HOW HAVE YOU CHANGED?

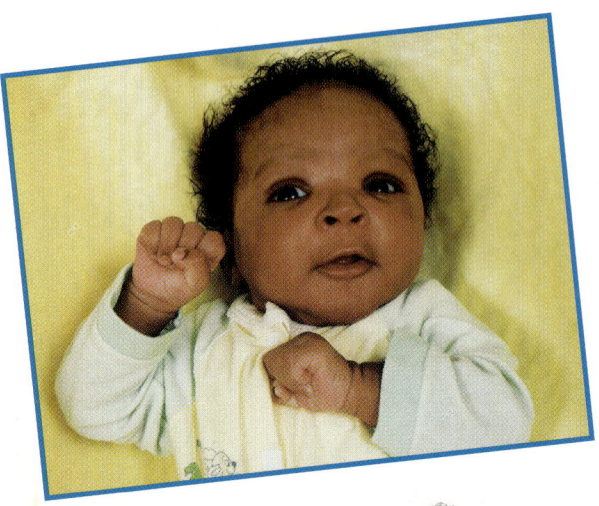

When Michael was born, he could cry and wiggle.

When Kayla and Kia were little babies, they learned to sit up.

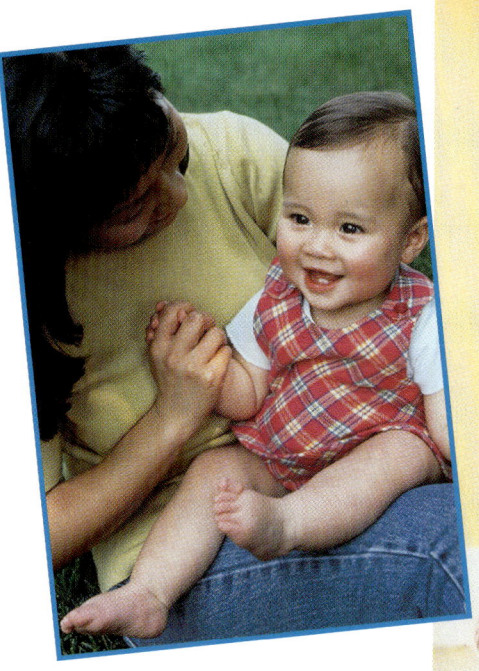

When Jonathan was seven months old, he got his first tooth.

When Jasmine was eight months old, she learned to crawl.

When Jason was a year old, he learned to stand and walk.

19

When Frank was three, he could run fast.

When Diana was four, she wanted to learn to tie her shoes.

When Amy was five years old, she learned to ride a bike.

As you grow, you can do more and more.

You are always growing.
You are always changing.

Changing is part of you.

 **How have you changed?**

REVIEW
Book 1

Wrap-Up

1 How are we all special?

2 How is a name special?

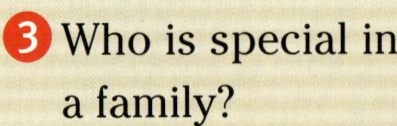

3 Who is special in a family?

4 What can children learn as they grow?